is(ness)
Copyright © 2025 Crisosto Apache

Original Cover Art by Crisosto Apache, "Ex-euphoria" (1990)
Author Photo by Todd Andreff

The font used is Times New Roman

Gnashing Teeth Publishing
242 East Main Street
Norman AR 71960
http://GnashingTeethPublishing.com

Printed in the United States of America

ISBN 978-1-966075-03-5

Non-Fiction: Poetry

Gnashing Teeth Publishing First Edition

is(ness)

— For my father Alfred Al Platero, who never stopped looking for my brother and me.

Preface

The future already exists, the past already exists, the present exists, and the dream world (imagination) exists. If I stand still, I exist and have experienced, am experiencing, will experience, and continue to experience and perceive all four dimensions of time in a moment. The importance of time and presence in a place of "is" captures the moments in stillness like a photograph, a painting, or a piece of writing. These moments of stillness create poems that project time and memory expressed in the self-offering meaning of my existence. *is(ness)* supports the quality and concept of momentary perspective. The vision behind this book is that poems represent a "meaningfulness" quality of presence or moments in a poem. What the poem is "about" in a state of existence as it "exists" without retribution or containment. The poems in *is(ness)* at times feel complicated because of how poetry or art is interpreted by "others." What is chosen to exemplify in this book is a concept where the poem "is" a poem that "is" about what the poem "is" about in a state of "meaningfulness", presence, and moments.

Place and the occupation of space help the realization of poetry. Recognizing language and imagery can exist together. How these ideas blend can outline the image of how the language is delineated in the poems. Recapturing the moments can be utilized to redefine the meaning of what is happening in a poem and the influence of the poem's imagery. The language and imagery in this collection have an abstract dream-like quality and are expressed in each poem. The reality of influence and experience is difficult to reimagine because those experiences can be triggering. Facing my truth through each poem and questioning those experiences is what I attempted in the poems. This is a new direction for how these poems were created. Direction has been important in my life and comes from basic principles of life direction, and ceremony from my culture. Direction defines how a person should walk in life. The poems in this collection are organized in these four directions beginning with the East.

East [wake] starts with the eyes opening and greeting a new light. The light is renewal and nurturing. *The Sun, Moon, and the Dead Raven* by d.g. okpik reminds me of Indigenous creation stories that explain relationships for the way things are and why I am given purpose. Over time I have come to appreciate those stories addressing purpose and wakeness. Often in my life I have lost my way and needed to be reminded of why I exist and to find meaning in my life. d.g. okpik's work does this for me for why these stories exist.

South [arrive] is the arrival. The South moves and directs in a clockwise motion leading to the West. When I think of the southern direction and moments of arrival, T. S. Eliot's *Little Gidding* comes to mind. Returning to a beginning is what I have done many times in my life. I am convinced I will never finish the work, particularly the writing. Returning to many of these poems is a beginning, or an arrival, even if that beginning has already begun. The poems have become cyclic. Just because I have added these poems to a collection does not mean they are conclusive. It means they have arrived.

West [dream] includes sleep and promotes dreaming. Thinking of Mary Oliver's poem *Sleeping in the Forest* has led me to evaluate dreams, which are abstract and define many directions of the poems in this collection and subsequently depart from reality. There are moments in my life where I have connected with the natural world through a hike or a drive in the mountains, often sitting among the trees and rocks. These moments left me vulnerable as I observed how influential power exists in nature. I also do not take it for granted. Even the movements through my urban surroundings, the city I live in, or driving in a car for long distances, sometimes through the plains influence poetry. The life happening around me never lets me forget how small and insignificant I am against the world's immensity, even in sleep, leading to the North.

North [depart] also represents the latter part of living or life which looks at life in the future, a departure from the real into the "other" or "beyond" capturing the imagination of an outward existence. *Time as Memory as Story* by Simon J. Ortiz is a poem that speaks of that existence as a residual concept of leaving my stories behind. Learning to understand my life connects me to places of my experiences, thus turning them into written stories after I leave this world. Time has always been against me, and I started taking my writing more seriously later in life pressures me to think about how much more writing I still have yet to do. In the later stages of my life stories are all I have to offer. I have had the honor to hear many stories and to add them to my own experiences good or bad. Many of the stories speak of survival through those experiences. Hopefully, these stories continue to move forward — ongoing.

Capturing a moment has always been important, especially in poetry. Many poets are interested in narrative, language, imagery, place, time, and positions. Photography captures time in situations, presence, locations, and history. Photographers such as Ansel Adams, the historical aspect, Robert Maplethorpe, the sexual and confrontational, Roger Ballen, and the abstract of people and place, and finally, Joel Peter Witkins who questions the mortality of body and the beyond. Painters capture the imagination of what can be interpreted. Painters such as Zdzisław Beksiński, a Polish artist, Dutch painter Hieronymus Bosch, and surrealist artists Joan Miró or Salvador Dali have influenced these poems. Religious ideation and influences from the Bible (KJV) are also part of the experience historically, spiritually, and psychologically. The book of Revelation is one such example. Utilizing the views in the enigmatic Book of Revelation to persuade the choices of moral obligation through damnation is part of the experiences in these poems. Looking at many of these moments of expression helps catapult the imagery in each poem where the experiential indigeneity of my existence is defined giving the work the much-needed attention and molding them into motion of the past, present, future, and "the afterlife."

EAST [wake]

"When it became daylight after the eclipse, the Sun went back home with a new husband, the Raven, from visiting her brother, the Moon; the Sun gave the dead man life by warming him with her rays of red like the out layers of willows." d.g. okpik, *The Sun, Moon, and The Dead Raven*

A Prayer for Us

our song is sung to the eastern mountain
our refrain remains inside a newborn
in spring chirping flickers push the quiet song
and we belong among the morning air

our song is sung toward the southern mountain
our youth in playful poise levels the afternoon
and heightens the yellow grasses, our children
build the frames of arbors holding the trees together

our song is sung to the western mountain
our drumbeat demands the consent of ancient
elders reflecting the knowledge and holding better
ways of life that carve the strength in our voices

our song is sung to the northern mountain
our cries echo through the looming slow fog
and waiting in valleys is the ash spreading
on frozen ground to muffle the somber sighs
— and heavy sounds

Calm

an unlocked door is open and hints at a greeting
of moist whispers made from the mild autumn air

dusk doles out a caress of soft emanating breeze
that engages the infinite motion of the nurturing sky

        —I am calm with a tiny tremble

clean wisps of slow swirls work their way over
the cascading juts of ancient snowcapped constructs

a small gust engulfs the mountainous space like burlap
decay as raindrops linger abiding temptation from the sky

        —I am calm with a tiny tremble

minuscule water droplets descend in a thrust of tumbling
cloud masses as the mist undulates the ever-changing

molecules gyrate dissolving melons inside my mouth.
autumn trees flicker in the embers of the burning twilight

        —I am calm with a tiny tremble

a bluish plight of abundant heaven complicates the scenic
sights capturing the luster of golden serrations in my hands

outstretch boughs of aspens glean the sea of yesterday and
reminiscent reflection of stars becomes a window theater

        —I am calm with a tiny tremble

the encapsulating height of mountains reminds me
        —I am on a balcony at dusk in Estes Park, CO

Born for Thorax

                           – tonight
beneath a cluster of stars,
they are born
emerging from their tightly woven pouch

under a dim light
of a thousand wicker specks
they march, up to the highest point
and jump   off in single file,

a microscopic battalion
of eight-legged   paratroopers
descending gallantly

disseminating from a red chili pepper
a palace made for dangling and swaying
                                    away
from their thin strand
                        of woven curtains
scaffolding to the rooftop

attaching to an impressive umbilical cord
unaware of their shimmer
                        in the moonlit peril

when pulling the last cord
they scamper into valleys and crevasses
        like tiny silhouettes
                            scattering
like a broken hack of black beads

emerging from their exquisite cocoon
they continue the dance and dangle

on a trapeze flight   flittering
without a doubt until the early morning

when dews consume the skeletal structure
                            —and wean

Orchid Moon

in the lull of an evening veil,
your face appears as an apparition
your hand lifting to a tide
of Moon Orchids

high in a mountain canyon,
sleeping underneath an aspen grove
with the intent to ease the release
of a reluctant memory

breezes may exhume my mind
but not like the impressionable
confidence of your caresses

doubt still lingers upon my skin
along with the insurmountable death
you carry inside your blood

one day when I wake
from my disregarding slumber
I will notice your body bearing
that silhouette garb

the sound of crushing gravel
beneath my feet disturbs
the soft radiating orchid petals
cringing beneath the moonlight

I am reminded of lunar displays
inside folds of opaque petals
–blink one eye and the moon is there
–blink the other and it disappears completely
–slide of fingers on both eyelids
        views the moon in all its brightness

in this perpetual gaze upon this moon
her light shines upon these forbidding eyes

– I then become her

Tonight

tonight, fists come pounding down!

the night sky reveals a distant eye
around the corner, the hideous kick
and strike our bodies there

the jolt, the clinch, the gasping of air,
the hideous leave us weak while
we make gurgling spurts
                              —a dire sound

from the gun barrel, possible sparks
then possibly expels a round,
and possibly misses our heads behind
the convenience store on the corner
of Cerrillos and Don Diego in town

a release of blood and a grunting flare
those fists come pounding down!

the hideous repeat their frantic actions
and pound our skulls into the ground
we who lay inert on the wet gravel

with a look of hatred, the hideous bare
each fist and beat our faces with despair
and define a kind of persistent unnatural
                              —dire sound

tonight, fists come pounding down!

Bruise

becoming the bruises
that mark my face

a flesh stain from time
with a gun in his hand

weighs a chance to lose
as the blood pools beneath

becoming the bruises

by a battery of hardening fists
thrashing by the shadow of two

a time of trust cannot be won
marking my face one by one

for a surging time is to come

becoming the bruises

Come On Up to the House
for G.L. Casey

a taillight glows red
                and my pulse escalates
under my skin accelerating with an evening sky
into a motor rhythm
           arms excel as two figurines in the pine trees
leaning against the stars
          towards greater heights and copious light

approaching fast and forward
                    closing the deepening clutch
of skin   shuttering a desperate embrace

that night I slept restlessly   the wind moaning outside
in widening haste   awake gazing at a disposition
sensing a need for hollow company
          your body is not similar to mine

hearing a word in sleep, hearing the word break
and senselessly acting on the word   as though the action
can be still   inside the words for a long moment
maybe holding in one second   —lasting

      on a windowsill, a crystal shard spins
four months pass   and desires rotate slower
into a confusing fragment   distorting the twist
      of brilliance reminding me
of the questionable proposition   the night we met

tossing inside the thistledown fabric   akin to linen
two conjugating configurations   fusing in an unnatural
leg lock becoming   two awkward ballerinas twirling
                —unnaturally in chime

each entangling notion   holds a relentless position
an amalgamate figure eight   of two clutching bodies
keeping each from our cambric linings

                        determining gazes
only creating vacant cardboard shadows lurking
again, against the bluish panels of the night-laden canopy

the body weakening   arms losing their flagrant grasp
feeling the air dangling against each body
                                consuming an opulent
                    spectrum
throwing each fusing section against the wall again
                                dizzying for a
                    moment
dazzling   hitting   the floor in a dull sound
feeling the weight of the words   breaking upon each body
mumbling again
                        —*come on up to the house*

On Speaking
after William Carlos Williams

in the morning, I wake

to such a daunting task

as the minutes pass, time proceeds

the coffee
—hissingly   — brews
—waitingly   — breaths
                    out from the spout

the alarm discerningly beeps

my last effort to move the bones

upwardly   — falling
          — upwardly — falling
still staring at the ceiling

lost in a dull gaze
          my thoughts are awkward

the regret is
          once I am awake
                    and moving about

                    — I begin to speak

San Francisco, California 1962
for my mother

      —she is a brave young soul
from an Indian reservation in New Mexico
never dreamt of leaving the lush green arms
of her tribal land feeling secure among
the scatheless air, where roads gravel always leading
her heart and blood rushing toward home

      —she is a brave young soul
playing with her rabbits in the summer
at her grandma's house and spending time
with relatives and running off with cousins
to El Paso & Juarez being stranded
and returning home greeted
by a strap that scared horses

      —she is a brave young soul
traveling to San Francisco in the fall of '62
with her aunt Birdie, cousins Tweedy,
Cucumber, Crow, Roderick, and Norman
arriving in the calm of the night where she welcomes
a broad array of oceanic smells and city noises
far away from the whispers of the pine trees
living among darker people, in Berkeley
a neighborhood where the city remains constant
making friends with black city block kids
and sitting beside them on public transit
and classrooms blending into the same colors
trying to feel safe walking along the evening
light as the winter mist presses on from
the apartment walls where James Brown echoes

      —she is a brave young soul
seeing in China Town lanterns dangling in a shop

thinking she had traveled to a different country
spending Christmas without gifts that year
receiving the memory of a million speckling lights
remaining with her until old age, telling her son

        —she is a brave young soul
walking across the Golden Gate Bridge dazzling
at the incredible height and slight swinging
looking at ferries beneath the massive bridges
and gasping at the immensity of the water surrounding
her, gazing upward watching herself peer over the queasy edge
becoming entangled by the views of decorative nets
swirling of gulls and pelicans, riding the trolley
zigzagging through the steeping streets of the city
smiling at the cars swiveling at the end of the line
who sings the tune to *San Francisco's Treat*

        —she is a brave young soul
returning in the early fall of '63 to the safety
of her mother who missed her embrace
returning to the smell of wood stoves warming
through the solid green meadows and valleys
returning to the beginning when young girls
are transforming into the sacred women
returning to a memory of folks living in San Francisco
returning to revisit her inward journey remembering
the cyclic times of each passing year
returning to remember a great man killed
in Dallas, Texas saying, *the fall of '63 was a sad time*

        —she is a brave young soul
whose memory remains with her beyond old age

SOUTH [arrive]

"We shall not cease from exploration,
and the end of all our exploring
will be to arrive where we started
and know the place for the first time." – T. S. Eliot, *Little Gidding*

Wake
after Zdzisław Beksiński [1929-2005]

the body   is a fool to sleep
—wake
—wake
—wake

now   time snaps back
now   time slivers down

in the moments of a fitful sleep
the whispers of the dead call

the dead do speak of deceitful anointers
the dead know the unaccountable fingers

the voices ravage and strip the body
by those building ash houses shifting in the wind
by those snaring visions of territory & ownership
by those erecting skeletal cathedral structures
        into the sky gaining access to some Kingdom

making lovers of combat and waking the violent tinge
uttering their Holy name full of an urging doctrine

deracinating provisions leaving a lost lineage
of beautifully rendering bones crisscrossing
beneath the dirt where their pious condemnation
                           remains

still compressing the malignant urban sprawl
malevolent victories of the past are the violent nature
leading the future masses into a meandering delusion

the body is a fool to dress in fine funeral garments

—wake
the pinching stench of stale perfumes and clinking
glasses of libatious odors floating about
cigarette smoke leering upon the body with the inhibiting
dry glazing eyes folding unto themselves forming
opaque bowls of pearl

cauterizing a cadaver as a loss of self-identity
for many to disinter and examine archeologically
remembering a corpse is and only exists as erudition
in a still frame away from the fragmenting light

a carcass does not divulge any information
of existence or personage
    —their bones hum
    —their bones murmur
    —their bones absorb
inside grips of gluttonous palms of archeologists
digging
            digging up
                    the resonating history
holding secrets of attraction of heaving flies
hovering toward invalid bodies   as the bloodstones bleed
   —stone   — blood   — rock

tilting in the views   lingering like the moments
when bodies plummet to the ground draining
from their falling flesh and staining the waterways
ocher   sending the messages downriver
filling into the camps of the encroaching enemy

the intruders dismiss the masses   the thieves laugh
the papacy   gawks and leaves a continuation
of camps wandering in place of the enemy
      forcing
      merging   not remembering

in all calculations of salvation
in all possessions
in all the world not worth having

      — if but a memory of a beaded medallion
is found   the stain of blood remains

if defeat is not embedding the stars
if defeat cannot be abolished
then identity is simply lost among the burying mounds
becoming the fool and laughing at the joke
         and remaining in the obscure dream
         silting in each hand

*And he [was] clothed with a vesture dipped in blood: and his name is
called The Word of God... [Revelation 19:13]*

Remnants

Standing as a man. Reaching into his shirt pocket and finding a used booklet of matches. He lights one for his cigarette. Tossing the hot stick on the highway near Albuquerque. Fearing the snowy season is near he continues walking toward the Sandias.

Later, walking past a cemetery in Albuquerque where gentle breezes are blowing. Kicking a small stone off the asphalt thinking about the dry Rio Puerco. He doesn't know why the river will never run again. Turning around he sees the cemetery and wipes his brow. Cupping the sweat in his hands and flinging it towards the roadway.

Tar layers and pebbles grumble underneath his feet and against the road. All he knows is the sight of an endless highway that does not end. Four directions surround him. He sees ants collecting parts from an old carcass while he waits for a ride to stop.

— living for no one. His home is beneath him.

Ha'úú'ą / Sunrise

the sun rises as any other sunrise
a light speckling at the end of a tunnel
a light caressing knuckle needlessly

to say yesterday's light
                is not yesterday
as in the day before but the lost days
of the dust settling   in the wind

tires slapping the asphalt cracks
slapping upon the road surface
      as a long song dispels

the light is not driving this body away
or vanishing that body
            more like retelling
the memory of my life's memory
or the movement of my wrist
or the location of my vessel lost behind the light

each morning driving towards
the sunlight   waking in sunlight
each morning   the light
hiding the shadows of mountains
that are supposed to always remain
there on the horizon   –always

every part of my life passes through light

the longer I live out here in the shadow
in the urban sprawl reflecting structures
my body sprawls outward and away from
          — the people of long ago
and the light shines less as them

                    and lesser upon me
the light still striving to caress my body
but somehow the elongating shadow
                    always captures me first
lost in the ruins
                        of an elapsing penumbra
against the western point of the horizon
where the home of thunder and lightning
                            –persists

and the face of the East greets them each morning
and every morning, always running toward them
                — the people of long ago

only wanting them to save me
                    from my solitary flight
and keep me tapping this hollow body
            saving me from this limitless endless run

Dyad

emerge	weep
out of	deceit
	for me &
the ground	when &
where	I roll by
a sprout	
does grow	& weep
to burst	for me
through sod	as I
through turf	rise high
below	reap
the soil	for me
the surface	as I
have shown	might die
for a promise	and sail
as light	my eyes
as warmth	and sight
by the sun	to the sky
one day	I may die

Creating Golden Heliotropes In Her Hands

palpitating into thunderheads

building the sky tonight   wide and tall
as myths in sheer black garments

the smell of electric pulses
tells us how far we are from her position
and how fast her heart will beat

with her shroud   she complicates
the evening with hues of rose   coral, and rouge

completing herself with moisture
inside her lips
          and inside her body

she glides along the hillsides
along with the pale grasses   swaying
her gown toward the pink horizon

gazing over mesas
and melding into mountains
as a jigsaw segment   fixing and jagging.

this evening, she finds the gaps
in extending hands
while making fists   pounding
and waving wildly inside her watery veins

assembly of aerial structures in the evening sky
becomes a particulate blur with rising ocher dust

in the distance   racing off
to the mountains   crashing into them

with great momentum   a non-stop collision
of water draining into culverts and waterways

she then dissipates as a haze in the distance
just below the Sangre de Cristos
disavowing everything and standing cold
fluttering under the feet of lumbering trees
imminently gazing toward the dusk of the earth
leaving a yellow desert flower   blooming

Momentary

a Pinacate beetle crawls   away from
or proceeds toward   the middle
of the asphalt with no destination or a place

the wide-open grass plains
moving at millennium speed
               with the furthest position
the Sangre De Cristo Mountains
moving slower and seeming to stand more still

against the black petroleum stripe
          the lengthening plain moving longer,
also having no destination or place
             — each object, each perspective
rotating at fifteen to twenty-five feet intervals
causing a winding motion of strings
             attaching to the left-hand side
sliding under the utterance of musical notes,
the music does not last forever
             nor do the knots
tying beside finger
          intertwining between fingers
             bleeding

the fluid moves water-like in my palm
and begins twitching in my hands and on my face
the movement across the plains
progressing the air   sweeping across my face
once moving forward, twice fighting back,
             also not lasting forever

a peculiar projection through sound
finding my ear in a high-pitch scream
gazing back   waving unconditionally

strains of some begotten memory slipping down
onto my lap as I remember my father
finding him in my old journals
will soon be laid to the new fires
of that old grey stucco house on the hill

finding next to the house   another memory
hiding between two old cottonwood trees
where wisdom protects me
from those spiraling emotional flames

in a heap of recollection, my finger leaves a streak
of sangria tears from flowing
— never forgetting

my face   my mouth   my eyes
traveling faster
shifting faster
moving this body,
underneath the wide grass plains
moving longer and less still
like the auric snag in my hands

recalling every moment   a modification in motion
wiping the saturation from my face
losing a recollection
of my mother's and father's faces
continuous and flowing within my fingers
persisting and lasting against
the form of the Sangre de Cristo
and Santa Fe is only thirty miles away

Long-Distance Traveling

killing a tick for the sake of a disease
can be more interesting than a virus
resembling an imminent threat
or having a reason to drink
water from a rushing stream.
        I am less fearful of dysentery

breezes settling upon spruce and aspen
wading through dead trees hindering
the way and swaying in a shift
of constant flowing water
                — fading

hollow logs   dense trails
falling leaves   sifting sun

sun veils passing clouds slicking the consistency
of water slipping from my hands full of sand
and comparing the slide to my life
the particles filtering away and always drifting
                      behind

my fingers swell like satin, unable to sustain a form
misting upon my breath
        I am losing myself again
vigorous as the inertia in my drive
        keeping me from moving forward
traveling south in the absence of affirmation

many silhouettes wander beyond my view
and I continue to be unaware of the tribulation
in the leaning crest of each mountain
wishing to become those jutting peaks
           overlooking

each ravine is a row of land furrows
or the aligning fibers of my empty hull
                    moments of indiscrete poise

as malignant, this adoration consumes
the further I drive the fermenting excitement
that seems to dissipate over the years
                    of losing you.

the distant scenery holds a distraction,
scattering the night with insects
that scintillate inside the indifference
of space and intertwining light

the anticipation beckons and is more dangerous
                    now than the last night

windshield wipers flick back and forth
saturating my eyes with every drop
pounding the windshield and distressing
the drive that impales my insignificant skin
suggesting a supple act
                    prevailing a blind man
against the blast of rain
                    dissolving his structure

in the haze, recalling a dragonfly resonating
on a granite slab and splashing water from its wings
hisses through the pilfering dust of Ponderosa pines
junipers and aspens

the repetitious flutter impacts and erases
                    the wet congestion of spaces

driving faster and dangerously contesting
                    the dazzling drizzle of questions

of an empty bed when I arrive seeking your company
but always a bit too late
with a natural caress of the pounding membranes
in my chest, it diminishes the salt
                    collapsing my cold vessel
                    and not recovering there

remaining in a bath of solitary vacancy, submerging
remaining under the influence of writing verses for you

sensing an aqueous presence but with each glance,
                                        there is absence
years pass and I can still smell you on my skin
but the scent is growing faint and lost

a ghost flower grows on my follicle edges
an apparition of skin projects a two-step cavorts
behind the wisp of a name that remains
                    a stain upon my muttering refrain

thunder clouds   sage brushes
wild horses   accumulate

the clouds passing and revealing a time
where we both sat on the edge of a tattered bed
these memories are an elusive ray of the sun
                    trying to reach my heedless face

One day I will not go through small towns
One day I will not be that contemptuous
One day I will not be trapped in muddy embankments
          or meander the low-hanging telephone wires

seventy miles an hour   abruptly stopping
Plymouth Omni in a ditch   engine droning

the wind releasing a soft draft one evening
in Vaughn, New Mexico
believing a myth can mimic a moment
      a horse was hit and killed moments before
remains a burdening shroud of any disease
                and apart from death
I unknowingly may be killing those nearest to me

Snow Falling In C Minor

again, finding myself inside my old mouth
a reluctant reminder of me as a little boy
now stuck as a ridiculous fortune of a fool

the downfall is a sensuous but trickling sweat
settling on the neck and back blades
as snow falls from the bleating city sky

stepping inside, trying to escape the cold New York
streets near Bedford & Christopher Street

the bar door opens into the heart of Greenwich Village
unleashing a masculine air, and leaving a slick
reminder inside the heart of (I) a little reservation boy
        — waiting for time to waste away

entering a bar in a non-conspicuous manner
and not in an inspiring way but bold as a baggy calm
welcoming the heavy pestilence where petulance
& peeve do not equally offer grudge or resentment

weaving in and out of tree lines the day before
in Central Park, waiting for the skies to open
and to confirm the small gathering of men, beneath
the looming leaves, meandering among the small
inviting nooks, before entering a shady plumage
of alcoves and muddling witnesses crouching
beneath the hedges, where curious silhouettes linger
among the thickets
        — a fumbling consideration of attractive devils

the afternoon settles, following a hazel-eye
around the city through the forgetful streets
not knowing if the streets truly lead anywhere

outside a precarious shop, exiting a taxi
with no comfort but the scent of a mouth
still loose in the hands of a bestowing gesture
through the magazines or dilatory redolence
of men ever lingering, and the protruding parts
      — always traveling

down a hallway towards a facet of pamphlets,
in this room   resting under a shelf
hangs the stench, the touch of a desirous drunken
stupor, finding a life in a violent endless whisper
                — a song

discover an adulterating touch is easier than sleeping
on my mother's sofa, or inviting strangers to sleep
in his bed even if the choice was a selfless act
      — desperately trying to keep the blood clean

making a phone call today as the mist falls
spending long hours, still thinking of a time
in a desolate house off the shores of Duxbury
walking about the rocky grey and sullen beach
            — redolent of
the fine slate sands, and the sounds of seagulls,
the temperature falling along the building pillars
the mass invasive people on this granite island
the igneous massing beneath a solid memory
the sienna stains on an old war photograph
the arms spread wide in a fluttering splay
the falling means, or reminders of suicide
the remnants of his lost friend on a car hood
the friend who had the potential of an amaryllis
but discovers a defining need to descend untouchably
the offspring
the parents

the partnerships
and cohesion
    — to say, *there is*
    — or to say, *there never is*
     or, maybe, *it is* just best to write porn
     and live a little

— loss
sometimes searching, sitting up at night waiting
displacing someone who will be part of this body
similarly resembling a mirror on a wall as a broken
reflection, along the way and always turning
with every breath etching on the smooth surface

this yearning keeps gazing, uttering the screams
through the beaks of a thousand Waterthrushes
and Warblers breaking the seasons, allowing the frost
to meld with the setting autumn and burning spring

after some time passes, with

no reflections
no desires
no recollections of the beginning
only seeming apparitions of lost separations as the snow settles softly
    — Rachmaninoff's apparition
    — the notes stay as distortion
    — *Vocalise* is not embracing
the child
the parents
the spouse
remaining in C minor
    — the realization of time pulls me forward
    — the snow falls silently just out the window

Always Asphalt
for my father

I always leave one place and move to another,
not knowing the endless cracks in the roadway

never becoming the scruples of caverns connecting
the lines on both palms and the millimeters of miles,
to sense only the imposing grip upon the rubber

remembering the day, the moment, the minute
of forgotten places
                   — or the willingness to drive —

the undulant motion spanning more than thirty years
and always encountering brief meetings that
preclude generously as exchanges of affection
          — ending, always leading back
          — a thirty-year unpleasant reminder

the transplantation of place and motion
fosters memories of a dream, from earlier
years to an unsettling moment before my birth,
during the colonial era, as a woman recalled
her grandfather's death, as an uncovered carriage
rolled by through the mud and recalled the details
of hidden experience, perhaps remnants of a
a memory, too far in the distant past, a vessel
stranded out on a lake, unreachable, unattainable

grief and longing pass relentlessly across
a barren landscape, counting a frayed canvas
and (I) a child remembering that female in a dream
and in sleep cried for empty inert kin and now
feeling the need to rejoin him

the recurring memory of distance translates
into diffidence of transmigration, and (trans)isolation
moving forward in the transportation of adapting
motion toward a state of acclimation, where there
is never a beginning or end to the lines on the road

later in history, a closer inspection uncovers a deep rust
of insipid water, encasing and exposing a liquid purple
near the surface of the skin,
        — a subject [the red people]
        — or an object [still, the red people]
pushing the process of the thickening blood
to a natural and insistent hour, passing the days
of generous visitations, where a blind man sits
sequestering on the edge of his bed

a 500-mile drive will not suffice for this belated homage,
and unchanging stillness of impressive unforgiveness

a ghost lays dormant inside a limbic curve, waiting for
the coming seasons of brown bottles wet in a grip

winter hides the frost caps of the Sandia Mountains,
where rose dust envelops the early morning

the almighty paint job   — unmistakable —
dream of a blasting 1956 Cadillac, shimmers
the shadow glistens on the reflection of the car,
shellac as champagne and turquoise against
the gaudy Chief Joseph upholstery

speeding toward Albuquerque, the memories
of a Blue Spruce, drunk on a looming bar stool,
reminiscing about the Cadillac speeding down
a dirt road, maybe on a Tó hajíílee pall of dust

and [origin of water]   — the wayward dream —

a journey of ascending off-ramps and construction
the music blaring, and the voice of rubber carnage

pounding the asphalt pulling the reservation line open
            — driving skillfully against an acculturative end

a vibrant vehicle, a state of mind after thirty-plus years
leaves me flitting in a turbulent blaze and dust particles

the engine rivets loudly rumbling in its fume
— vibration in my jeans
— ignition into flame
— sparkplugs bursting in time
— electric shroud falls upon the eccentric buzz

miles of unending miles finally come to a stop
            — halt of silence
            — the car never starts again
            — no fair warning
            — stranded and hissing
            — stuck on the open road
with an insatiable urge for a fix to finish the journey

ode to all the flexing gearboxes and shifting muscles
ode to all the sliding gears recoiling, cocking
ode to all the rubber carcasses on fiery asphalt
ode to all the fascinations of murmuring truck stops
ode to all the filthy streets and riveting back roads
ode to all the beer cans flying from crusting windows
ode to all hitchhiking along the dimming interstates
ode to all cigarettes littering the rising medians

            — in the rearview mirror, I am leaving
            — the image of a father moving to another place

Deeds Unbeknownst

for B. Quarterman

days last, in a haze, a simple lure in ways of decay,
fuels a vascular blaze into a wretched day of glory
                                        — August 8, 1998

1.

months inside sipping old coffee
sitting in a moment and conjuring a caffeine-stain
            — a moment existing anywhere

night succumbs to darkness eventually
and a consuming thought crosses my mind
questions the placement of my dolling hands
and positions them on a shoulder and face

such a grave movement inspires tragedy in men

lucidity overcomes each time these hands
welcome the silhouette on every street
watching, dissipate into mist, and passing
the waning moments and cold premonitions
            — still waiting, still anticipating

awake at night recollecting the daylight
the trees in autumn crepitate their leaves
remembering a recourse of crunching decay
beneath my feet hindering the chill of stale feelings

feeling every waking state that concludes the path
under the weight of shadows, inhaling and forgetting
the stagnant hardening breath and imagining
the suckling remnants of every bottle while young

crippling each night passing with a rippling trigger
with each momentary vehicle and oncoming stagger
each step hopes for a wayward ride, reminding each
fastening sway in each voice of father and mother

right before eyes shut the imprint widens the glare
where nothing pools but refraction, frightening
into segments separating the center or a body
disposing of bottles and deflating erections traveling
inside each escalating month of lonely rejection
going back to square one and reclaiming
an assortment of agitation behind eyelids
remember nothing of the gladdest days
just the confusion of filth steeping
in retribution for these secondhand shoes

on any given night alone discover in back alleys
a newly dim room with neon accents entering quietly
away from heaven as winter hits hard severing limbs
of old trees, only waking to find consciousness
one morning has blown away the scattering leaves

some days confusion seems greater than the pain,
inflicting the inside, skin on a helpless body
                — maybe, it was a long time coming?

throwing a stone is better than tossing it
because giving a stone meaning compares
to throwing an Apache child taught to enjoy
the stillness and thinking of places where the spirit
is free and the stale feeling under the skin is quick
with a whim of passage while in continuous captivity
meaning nothing as a captor to a prisoner, or a dying eye
                — as a ghost walking among the camp of the enemy

a journey always takes longer to a place of coincidence

a place of unrecognizable landmarks, a place connecting
causeways centering and outstretching as an isle of endless
grids and extending further into a meaningless distance
until the extension of self-concept fails to view itself

one day a beige woven glove rests on a step while walking by
those passing by do not notice this beige glove which becomes
an axiom, a reflection

2.

> *Remembering*
> *your smile*
> *your presence*
> *your gift*
> *your longing*
> *your story*
> *your unsettledness*
> *recalling the morning and leaving*
> *... only in strength*
> — September 25, 1998

en route to the other side of the city to a musty bar
where two old gentlemen sit inside the misty shadow

a momentary rut making a move to fall for anyone
who would fill a desperate spirit flesh-and-bone

unsettling skin drops beneath as tainting leather
each strap crosses each torso and lap binding
chest and limbs, placing the unstable glares of charging
fluid and eventual moves and untimely passages
of sainthood leading to an absolving and irrevocable
penitence marking the body in a perpetual stomatic state
                   — stuck eternally

a willing feeling and a willing silence persist

traveling hard and fast down the passageways
filling with content and no regret for this complacent
      — misguiding behavior

speeding from the luminance of this conurbation
no regard to the heart, carrying tightly between each arm
a misguiding blessing of purple milk thistle blooms

streetlamps gleam, passing as candle sticks
in the night or a maraud of angels marching at high speed

recognizing an urge to race for any unknown destination
the rubber burning on the asphalt and smelling
the intelligence concealing away in a rampant grip
taking on the first-lit liquor store in sight then the last
inhale of the chemical mist settling at first light
                                  — sunrise

observing the firm grip and sensation and blaming
the iridescent mood, accepting the irrelevant urge
to run, turning the starter switch, clicking the gear
into position, and sending the ignition into flame
nearly driving on the verge of a crime and driving deeper
the curse inside fingers and throwing carelessness in the air

racing to no particular destination or conclusive
fume or ash only a flaking flurry of affirming spirals
speeding down the oncoming lane in a hyper-sonic blur
leaving no time for picture-perfect moments or losing
in a Daguerreotype image of cross-dressing Christ in satin

speeding on Colorado highways at seven in the morning
and shifting light from indigo to flaxen on the vacant roads
of each county ending the night in the salvation of a red taillight

finding sanctity inside a mobile home, where one day
after leaving this large town's confidence is balled in a cloth rag
    — in some corner room

3.

> *draping in a silent slur*
> *of wardrobe, dubbing*
> *the cradleboard dreamer*
>   *...twinkling*
> — July 25, 1998

a heavy crown of thorns lying beside me
with legs stretched out, an example of foul extensions
of flesh, and muscle   a type of aggression exerting
the stretching movement of a skeletal frame, an eternally
burning flame to provide a conjugal mistake for two
reservoirs of bodies asleep in the same bed with all
the entangling years in a nostril, with hand over feet

pressing hard over every muscle while the candles dissipate
twice hearing the echoes of clicking and slurping sounds
an underlining assortment of miasma and glass pipes lost
somewhere among the smoke and clasp of desperate embraces
tangling bodies shuffling off in the bathroom and at the foot
of the lush beds and wanting to turn off each sound
resembling an exit for extrapolation and forgotten fools

twitching stomachs pinch and recognize the insatiable
thundering bones from healing each sticky drop
of condemnation, and masquerading confrontation
swirling their way into twilight contaminating the images
of Christ in drag and flickering the indecency that spooks

dawn approaches again and the kindling crackles
in the remnants of the night's fire collecting the loose bodies

— now nowhere to be found

howling dogs from underneath the trailer houses with their
mistaken assortments of profuse snarls

pushing the mouth and spit into drying walls
cracking a desire to split with a flustering toss

so early morning and in between heaven tossing nearly
to some stemming utopia and the long night's wake

a conclusion of stars spread across the admiral night sky
sleeplessly inside each eye where nails never touching feet
        — estrange
        — unraveling

4.

> *serious departure*
> *away to gather bruises*
> *tossing them to the sky*
> *and losing the soul inside*
> *... the day is anew*
> — January 3, 1998

always gazing upward at a star-struck ceiling, a crystal
hanging globe is in exaltation with mosaic patterns
scattering throughout and thinking of numbers in two
        — undoubtedly, still alone

every evening the differences in configuration between
each sheet becomes the same contour and the only
common denominator sensing no time and slipping out
of a chest of drawers where nothing seems to happen or change

the candles flicker relentlessly as the anger conceals

packing in my bags with no way out of this frail trailer frame
only tunneling passages beneath the slat of the backdoor

finding a sleeping body on the couch with an ash-crossed forehead
oddly remembering nothing of a heartache or religious holiday

a scathing lapse of reason and the remnant scar lining
of a previous smoking habit and the trailer is empty

no quiet distinction of conscience
no recognition of sub-conscience
no recollecting picture in hand
no ungodly wasteland of gravel roads
   — no expedition to expedite
   — unconquering
life carrying gusts of wind and whimsy uncaring for the world
noticing trashy strips of asphalt, empty cars, and smokestacks

long black strips of the roadway and corroding railroad tracks

traveling across the landscape with anticipated derailment
acknowledging judges circling over the land
waiting for a timely descent onto carcass, bone, and body
banishing a novel flickering motion beckoning the lights
dismissing the fast descent and ever-slowing circular motion

no time seemingly unknown still listening for the conjurer
the ones who flee the scene and devour with delight
the ones who search inside each scintillating flight
and sitting alone waiting for an awakening lost child
of its homeland and returning to the night sky
heading westward southbound, into the moon
descending through daylight, like a withering blossom
      — again, unknown

WEST [dream]
"[...] All night
I rose and fell, as if in water, grappling
with a luminous doom. By morning
I had vanished at least a dozen times
into something better." — Mary Oliver, *Sleeping in the Forest*

Illusion of Dreams & Existence

Driving home, I fear the dream may happen again. A child crosses the road and stares at me. Looking at my own hands, trying not to look up. I do. Does the child exist? People cross the street. My arm hurts. Scars run up, dividing the skin into shallow rivers of broken elastic bands. People intertwine into moving shapes strobing in the sun's immaculate light. The street is clear, and the child is the last to cross. Does the child exist? Rolling down my window. Cool air dries the sweat off my forehead. Driving past and stopping, hoping it isn't happening again. People cross the street and the child stares at me. Looking away and fighting the urge to look again. Does the child exist? Driving on. That night I slept. Waking to a strange noise coming from another room. Getting out of bed and walking down the hallway. Stopping in front of the bedroom the noise stops. Turning around and heading back to bed. In my sleep, I wake to the sound of a crying baby. Sitting up in bed and notice I am alone and then go back to sleep. In the morning, I rise and get ready for work. Sipping coffee, I hear a child laughing from the other bedroom. Looking in the direction of the door the noise stops. Does the child exist? Leaving the house, getting in the car, and proceeding to work. Turning my head and backing out of the driveway. In my periphery, I notice a child walking. Stopping as the child turns to me. Rolling down my window and asking the child's name. The child turns and runs. Continuing to work. Does the child exist? Driving my usual route home that evening and it happens again. On the way, stopping twice and seeing the child each time. I begin to worry about these visual reoccurrences. Does the child exist? That night I go to bed early. In the night I wake again to the strange noise coming from the spare bedroom. Crawling out of bed and walking down the hall. The noise stops near the bedroom door. Turning around and heading back to bed. The next morning, I wake to the sound of a laughing child. Crawling out of bed and noticing I am alone. Getting dressed and heading downstairs to drink coffee. From the kitchen, I hear crying coming from the spare bedroom. Approaching the door, and staring at the knob, the noise persists. Slowly swinging the door open and entering the room. Looking around. The room is empty. Turning around and exiting the room and thinking, does the child not   — exist?

Scarce Seeds: In Seven Parts

I. Light

technical creativity
combines with spasmodic light
and outbursts extrude inside the inner ear

seeing bad dreams about web feet, and
hands and holding a feather off Menaul Blvd
or could it be Central Ave

walking the street at night   peering
into woven tree limbs and windows detects
                ...what was said and what was not possible
                ... shedding in the darkness

II. Corridor

many nights exist of silent invasions

the clean hallways are awake and shining

skimming the slits in the eyes
down these long hallways to hear
the corridor doors   flutter in their sway

some ways down the lit stretch of white
some lights flicker behind a dimly etched
                                window panel

the motion inside is not pulsating but more
                                like gliding

while reaching for the sheets, the floor is left spinning
the floor spinning and spinning on the floor reaching

touching the angular feet and the postmortem skin
reaching for the roots of auburn hair
and finding each clump slightly matted

a female utters, "out there" with lies in her mouth

the neck muscle jerks on the windowsill
and flattens the skin against the barricading film

the fever persists in the jowls and swells intermittingly

others yell as limbs are lost in the wake
of an anesthetic lip hole to which there is pain
waking the comfort of grit underneath
the fingernail after the dirt settles in the trouser pocket

sitting at the window may remind the reflection
of what appears behind the transparent barricade
while staring at the image coursing inside the silhouette
inside the folds of the darkening hillsides

… the song of men is heard
sit among us
sit to our left
sit to our right
talk to us on either side

in corners, eyes begin to shift
fast, and recognizable on beds of fleeting fire

… door closes
… eyes shut
… sounds are loud
… footsteps remain outside

now   the light is not light   only confusion
of mass ceiling vibration and unending corridors

III. Daze

the morning threads the creasing agile skin
whispering they fold onto themselves carefully
to not disturb and show the unsettling scars

passing one moment where the eye does not watch
the chains jangling behind glistening doors

the sun is early
the time feels ever colder
the slumping mole reveals each shoulder

valves enter the mouth
sucking the sounds of suckling light
beam seals the door and the recourse divulges
                    … midnight after night

the light never recovers

the light may never work again
a picture of light hangs all about, all the time, all around
and the light seems the same for each

… home in a dream, will be within reach, soon enough

IV. Under

                  do not
touch   the skin
because   the skin touches
in ways that connect each dream
as valves and seals as real

interpretation as coils

… again, footsteps click down the hallway

V. House

lights come on late in the evening

they go out again   no one seems to know why
to enter the room or the house
they remain empty and always vacant.

the red beam wisps by while walking at a distance

VI. Cirrus

stooping down and staring into the yucca blossoms
recognizing a pattern seen in the sky the prior day
                    … a dream on a passing cloud

VII. An Opening for the Mountain Spirits to Secure the Agile Sorrows in
Palms

… the window   … of hands
… reminding the eyes to move forward
… lifting the latches
… and releasing him back to his homelands

Near To Nearer, A Foreseen Death

unusually born, emerging hard as a hole
upon a cliff top leaking ancient liquid
on an old, bloodstained garment

scooting limbs through damp motions
proving smaller and insignificant movements
and hanging taller than lumbering doorways

quailing mouths still speak occasionally
licking lips clean and again staining

the quaking mouths speak from old places
and under floorboards, growing vowels into
shifting cups thrusting backward building letters
on each nook and corner of basalt cliffs

crumbling stone sometimes grows tired of listening
to heavy drops of water in furrow pockets

visiting sediments sometimes erode
hearing the creak of newly laid rocks,
sitting helplessly watching thresholds
grow long mouths, becoming high-drenched
locations for old developments
                                        — older still

plastic forms stand on and rotating currents
lifeless hands never capturing the sky
never looking up at the convincing blue

disruption of the soil, plants, and land dissipates
as the waters die away from the natural color
learning to dislike the collection of splendid life

conceived unusually hard, life cracks the warring
hands offering feet direction sinking into plastic
linings that continue forward and contrived

there is no difference between ten years
and one hundred fifteen years
the years are the same as a decaying rate
add another twenty years to expose the bones

children are not yet aware of the skeletons
racing toward the hollow houses

they see themselves walking forward, walking forward
and never in the opposite direction
                — children will never stop the movement

suffocating in the air that forces fear into the rain
turning the backs of children who become the prophecy

ears are placed to the ground hearing the groan
of heavy bones writhing under the earth
singing songs as waves sway back and forth
turning the old squeaky ligament into a wailing sound

gathering by the thousands, by regions, forming
a full-scale circle waiting for an occasional fingertip
to thrust a lost embedded memory inside the mammary
glands of those desperate mouths

life isn't important to anyone sitting there at the table
life is simply a mathematical equation forming
within the pupil of eyes that find death easier
adding numbers to an increasing list and those
numbers will not bring the children back
                        — never
solving the endless equation of the infinite confusion

the opulent eyes find the sky again minus the red
color of birth igniting speckles of water on the ground
with a reflection hoping to cover a shame
where people no longer covet the earth
but becomes the reassurance of life as the inherited clay

Sun rays capture the [beauty way] and in the end
                              — the seeds prosper

Stasis
for Tommy

when the spores scatter, we catch the dust
in our nostrils, we catch each other looking away
while stretching out, and gazing out beyond the spruce
           — such a stumbling stare

sprawling under the spruce trees after the red-spotted
caps wilt stretching outward in a bluish star-stream
           —spraying across the ground
and the spores come settling again
with the low-hanging limbs and pricking seed pods
           —curving over an Auria of pitch
and sailing over and around our heads
       into reliquary
       into vascular
       into cochlea

sleeping   and sitting   we sit
flaxen and muted as needles break free and quietly fall
landing on our pleating backs and waxen calves
the surmise   the tickle from where I sit
           —an untouching coral

stirring   stirring   rolling onto our bellies
           —cold and damp

the sky rotates   the land rotates
the day rotates   and throughout   rotates

these bodies beneath the post office & adobe
me a silhouette   us a silhouette

time to slumber   time to reach   ever
with the remnants of gills vibrating in exhalation

        —always extending
soon it will be time to reach deep into the caps of our intention
and touch took so long to encumber the deepening ease

perhaps later, but for now we sleep   we sleep now
                —sleeping under the indigo sky

waiting all day for our eyes to recognize
ourselves high above   as a looming limb

Gemini [They/Us]

moving in one direction through an opulent frame
traveling upward and dissolving with the Earth's sky
observing the inside field of cornstalks just beyond

           ... a gravel roadway
           ... always the opposite
           ... always connects inside

a cottonwood slat splits along the warping grain
and into slivers   blinking through profuse eyes

in an intermittent connection with so much history
seemingly gnawing on a sapling, a small elm branch
in such a way, stripping the young periderm bark
from the inside exposing the energy of the stars within

Silver flakes spin off, trapping the lure in each eye
leaving a woven dream and threatening the bodies
into obscurity, while sitting and staring at each body

left behind is a sheet of glass, there on the dresser
a translucent image on an etched slate of glass

           ... on brocade a liquid silver

a warbling breeze outside, soft on the windowsill
behind fog panes, distills in four equal parts:

    I.   edges fold a line from each ear
    II.   written scripture in a loose grip
    III.   untold stories as celestial lore
    IV.   eyes lock inside the mouth

expecting the eye to notice palms pressing against
the face, perhaps for some missing vague reason
a clear notion of the body, staring at the stars beyond
the trees and in their way telling a story of two bodies

falling inside the rooms of an empty lavender house

the impression in each eye judders, an unnatural
position making the bodies lapse in a staggering action

the cottonwood frame falls off the dresser to view
how the stars would align over the expectation of time

we enter the house   the sheet of glass shatters
opening the cracks   revealing our hopeful embrace

last night we walked the two-a.m. route home
the quivering moon in our eyes spoke in our hands
working toward the body at the thought of us quaking

a quaking second, we make something happen
… we pull   … we throw   … we tumble
in our ears from across the room, we remain introverts
into the next night before we blend with the moonlight
expecting a litany of vowels, a volume of text spills
from the same words that come from our dry tongue
from the emotional (we)
                              … expose speaking prophetic charm

the pulling change and the will of our slippery skin
speaks of how we would leave through the Earth's sky
and never return to the night where we offer ourselves
to the unyielding belt of Pollux and Castor

we enter the house just off Gold Avenue and the city
moves on with the wishes of stillness and rotating stars
we hope the knock on the cottonwood door will invite
reassuring upon our return to the words "come and stay"

that night, we still move in one direction upward
but this time we separate and miss each other
                              … or maybe we never notice

Diminishing Spaces Between A Mouth

recalling another brief moment in a dream, where
                                a reverse word reverses
on the other side of the wall in an empty room
a pencil depicts a letter   a period
                          or perhaps a skull

recalling a man living inside the membrane
of spaces closed and away from faces
building structures with sandstone rocks
on the mesa top overlooking
                        the Santuario De Chimayo
                        remembering— the ~~Devil~~ in ~~God~~
recalling the red earth from the chamber
that once healed him from utterance

remembering the man who turns
a beam held within an absent room
where darkness flows up
                        — and never down
recalling the wind swaying against the rocks
and sand below calling out the name
and summoning the cries for a ~~Christ~~ on a hill

in the wide space of the night sky the light showers
hiding the stars until they cease to shimmer
catching the vacuum of the dying light
                        the fading light —
                        the fading light —

shadows dance on the other side of the wall
trying to resurrect the cursive soil
of energy emanating from the lead tip
the sandstone hardens over time
but can crumble quickly rejoining

the other sediment and restarting
the solidification process of pressure

time —   light —   tension —   silence —

all define the silhouette of the body of existence
trying desperately to remember

most of all he remembers, he is lost and darkening
in the syllables disassembling against the air

Moonlit Slabs of Light on a Hernandez Church Floor

after Moonrise Hernández, New Mexico *by Ansel Adams*

a cemetery

                                    is lit by the light

                                   of the moon, while time

                         stands seemingly still,

              lamenting a

          timeless value,

which covers the empty floor

          in the shape

                                  of a dying face,

the hollow bell knells solemnly

                  for the dead to linger there,

                  to be buried again

hollering is the reason for

                        the isolation of solidarity —

                          a tragedy

that befell the dead,

          the decaying reason has taken its chance

beneath a standing tree made into crosses,

the mountains are alive

                      yet the dead appear dead,

               there is no willful purpose,

while a fly sits humming on the sill

          and ants gather,

to confirm time is still ticking,

that light gleaming on the floorboards,

never ends the ceasing shadow   — but it does

                           — but that light

                           is beyond the dead

When I Follow Prairie Storms
written while driving across Kansas after a massive hailstorm.

1. catch

on a hill sits
a house
a dilapidating frame
broken windowpanes splitting shards
a weaving memory
falling sunlight in the morning

rumbling clouds in each gust
time enters the house
beckoning the fractures
dehydrating the floorboards
creating perforations
deadening the thunder
crying quietly

residual sounds of a crying child
slipping into the mouth of its mother
reaching for the nipple
fresh and historical

on a prairie hill
the house begins to sing
raindrops drench planks
matting dust holds stale blades of grass
wavering over the rigid reed stems

petrichor is fresh
kissing the lungs
deepening the shadow upon my lips
lingering within dark frames
waiting for possible fragrances

summoning sleeping clear dew
raindrops fall on the brow

curving inside a mirror reflection
shadows a slumbering twist
of a strange smile

the clouds turn gray,
ripples pass the yellow waves
within deepening eyes
running off the grass
brushing away the wetness
that covers the ground
mildly sounding the space
of breath and twisting arms

2. rupture

receiving kiss
falling to the floor
dilapidating forms of raindrops
scattering fragment about
the leaves in a hairline

gripping inside velvet eyelids
smearing vivid dusky streams
of vocable pieces
filling the room
uttering a minuscule "k"

pounding rain in vascular depths
pours down my ocular openings and spine
kneeling on limbs from a loosening body
turning over then under in the wet sod

mirrors reflect a murmuring delusion

of stale footsteps shattering
a child's cry holding a gasping breath
        — the fear of slumber sets in

flinging out onto the wasting sky
and through the grassy blade
 and through the cords of veins
singing lyrics of resentment and frustration

the revelry lingers over empty heads
looking toward the purple sky
feeling the rush inside swelling veins
the extension of nails hides under
red-stained fingers and the shade of skin
while the pouring water bleeds on a sleeve

transcending into the memory of hands

lifting to the whisper to the last raindrop
before the storm passes

3. release

        — goodbye

Random Thought Patterns / Anatomy of a Lipid Cell

it is Tuesday the 5th of September
— what seems like a train speeding by at 20 ft

the printer finishes the last page
— the sun is already out

a light beam drudge in
— source unknown

the sun starts red and then casts an orange shadow
a staunch projection of the future mounds in the desert

the shadows sway and merge
— fast and then faster
— printer diverges the first page

in a continuous dream, a vehicular memory emerges
— molecular swap meet

de-glu-ti-tion
— swallowing down, swallowing deep,
— a deeper gluttonous act
— an act or progress of swallowing

as-sim-i-late
— within the chest, starts a new day

sun-rise, in a continuous dream
— people enter and exit
— each eccentric in their light
— odd mingling behavior
— eclectic

love is rough, in a continuous dream

— no clouds in the sky
in a bathroom
— nighttime painful urination
— dreams during incarceration— nonsense

in a continuous dream
— extra-terrestrial, space, UFO probe
— nulls the cranial stairway on a high horse
— a golden saddle

atmospheric acid on the brain
— another cranial decadence

wedding bells, in a continuous dream
— why not?

sway and swish, in a continuous dream
only wanting to be held
— through conceit, through caress

squiggling, in a continuous dream
— among coils, pipes from some basement

gorgeous & amp, haughty in a continuous dream
— a body from a stretcher unleashing Orpheus

gathering orphans for an Opus
— a late-night musical persuasion
— not with three, love, coupling, or sheets

cars race at night in a continuous dream
— no carburetors, chains, or coyotes howling in heat
— some travel in packs and others travel without

Vaughn, New Mexico, in a continuous dream
— a small-town diner, a note says, that was beautiful

stars may bloom, and cars will swoosh
into a dark facade and affected by a sugar-high

it/I/you/he/she/is/am/are/will be hiding in a seat in the
desert

a lonely old man wants the company of the youth
steel brush scrapes unkempt tires
and only for one evening, there are tears

using an illustration of a cattle herd
and a drawn carcass full of colors

darkness is faster than all fingers
— anxious and speeding lying along the highways

wandering far in a continuous dream
— an audio file with an annoying tapping beat
— tapping on a surface with no direction
— a radio dial emitting static

red wine in a continuous dream
— a stoic bright moonlight serenade

one hour remains in a continuous dream
— until my/our flesh crawls together tight
— words cannot express enough
— the infatuation concludes at dawn, 5:00 am

Words from Foliage: A Miser Speaks

I. The Danger

it is dangerous ...
the old man says *when I get a hold of you*

water leaks on the floor, and the unreasonable
breakable bones and flaky skin

a caw in the distance thrusts enough sound
for a fist to defend a mood swing
the ammonia on his skin dries beside an aged spot

sleeping and dreaming of stale steps underfoot
and hearing milky whispers and low muzzling groans
tongue-twisting under and fizzes into a fistula

one eyelid closes under worn linen
at twelve a death watcher twitching and moving,
keeping the transformations from happening
inside the transparent sheets
it has been sixty-four years, and the eyes are opaque

midnight passes and the Death Watcher
conjuring his motions to secrets in hip flanks
and the old men in their beds stop moving

II. Quietness

silently counting the numbers on the floor
until the convalescent unit opens up
and the night bleeds inside veins and away from corneas
an unnoticing tiny metal ball rolls silently under the beds

waiting sympathetic as the watcher

does not hesitate, breaking between steps
each step is dizzying as the skid brings
bursts of brightness then dim again

exiting the quivering light, away from the shadows
and silence rolls through their stillness, unwavering

the grip is fast, clutching each handrail
whispering, and holding on, deciding to walk alone
the pungent ammonia air reminding each follicle
of a place where people don't show up

in one room the occupancy is quiet, in the other,
the hum of the dim lights and the pale squeaks
of good intentions

someone may walk in and see the heads
turning in their beds and at any moment
realizing there are more of them wincing

one eye always remains open, watching

III. The Light

immense radiance between settling dust,
nestling downward, into the realms of hands
reaching for each leg, sometime after midnight
a memory of the first night, when probes touch
the tips of fingers and deaden the feeling
and wake the shouts,
        — away from the face!
        — away from the body!

withering fingers stretch out into position,
geometrically fixing and then bending crossways.

lack of moisture in the skin rips all sensation
from the bed-stricken men who dream
unrecognizable dreams late into the night

mapping out their existence with their fists
their dreams remain unseen by the obscure daylight

waves of shallow shadows continuing onward,
the wisps of hollow men packing away belongings,
dragging belts, while in the other room, others wait
    relentlessly
      — *away from the face!*
      — *away from us!*

a metal frame catches a reflection
the faces are lost in a tubular position free-falling
and turning into a fist defending each mood swing
into eternal guttural glottal gasps

Self Portrait Before Candlelight

after Galway Kinnell

a window opens —   closes
a push of subtle air dragging the spine
while trying to wake

out of the periphery, a shifting eye moves
through the shadow of trees, behind
a transparent film, finding a threshold on each limb

a kind of motion, endlessly spinning,
a helix twirling up each spine
                    always —   fearing

the blood remains heavy, even now
before thinking of the father
                    always —   awakening

men cannot be careful enough to stop
the will of sleep

a motif of puzzling answers comes after sickness
                    always —   hearing

bending to such strenuous living or breaking
simple principles are meeting an aortic complexion
at point blank

the tongue still hangs in mouths sack-like,
preventing the seepage of breath.
                         no breathing —

here is emptiness, though made of flesh, blood,
bone, and meat
                    always —   poisonous

quickly dusk comes and the two stand in a room
made of glass shards reflecting among the star-scattering
sky waiting for a recurring sickness to speak
about the previous night

the two face each other in vibrating faces of war
attempting to maim one another each time they meet
the unwillingness to become second, standing
before each of their ever-looming presence
and the two will never sever

trembling across both minds and confirming
the existence of a cathartic chrysalis that says
                    you are not here —

ignoring the cricket wings chatter
and playing along with the idea they are simply
imagining a perception of any self-image

hearing the countless murmuring hearts
beating, throbbing, and bursting the capillaries
that flood the crown and never turn away

holding up every crystal object, knowing
at some point, each object will slip and fall,
creating a defying silence

spinning spaciously around the bodies
echoing the sound of silence
assuring the spread of red linings
kill each body
                    — always losing

tearing the linings from the skin and closer
to the distance of not far enough toward

the horizon but always close enough to cut

hearing the beating rhythms of old bones
cracking in age and red faces staring down
creating illusions of arms, lucid arms
                        — not embracing

rushing into dreams, chasing the uneasy strands
of hair locks, locking non-existing doors with padlocks
                        — closing
                        — open

dreaming of men in blue posing in pink beds, racing
for an ocher dawn, towards tomorrow's shady colors
of azure and white
                        — always self-destructing

bonding with quill and paper, ink dripping from the mouth
and standing on the edge watching, like a boat still in the water,
a wet grave, holding an identity calling,
                        — ice pieces

extensions contort inward, leaving the middle pointing up,
bringing forth the truths of the pen where each stroke
is choking on every call

palms wave over the edge of the whickering light, spreading
a conflagration of smoky images swirling outside the flame,
taunting a child unwilling to play

eyes blinking, blending into diminishing shadows of
perfect ghosts

eyes open finding fingers in eye sockets after seeing nothing,
only another person thought to exist

socializing means a beginning and also means forgetting
about the contours of the body, so Sebastian
                 — never speaking

separation sets houses of old things aside somewhere
in a thicket calling to new growth of forests and meadows

standing away   turning away   leaving behind
the burning wax ever waning

Enter Dreamtime

Stroll at Midnight —
A guy is walking inside an irrigation ditch during the night. He turns in time to notice and witness a large grotesque male strangle a young female child of eight. Upon hearing the guy walking through the grass, the strangler turns and gazes at the guy with vile contempt on his breath.

The strangler's attire stands out in yellow.

In fear for his own life, the guy runs into the darkness. The strangler chases him through the nearby thicket of taller grass. Without hesitation, the guy notices a tall fence and hops it without difficulty. The guy stumbles into a dirt roadway. In the distance, he hears an oncoming vehicle and sees the glare of the headlights. In relief, he is dimly aware that it is a patrol vehicle.

He is offered to be seated in the front, by the officer.

The officer says, "We have apprehended one of them." There is a mysterious figure sitting in the back seat, with a familiar voice saying, "I am afraid I must extinguish your subtle awareness of my action."

The figure seated in the back pulls forth a gun and shoots the man through the left temporal lobe. The bullet exits the top of his cranium. In fading, he hears the officer yelling at the person seated in the back seat, "I can't believe you did that!"

Child —
A man stands inside a house with white rooms. He is gazing out one of the windows. In another room, he hears an infant crying. He walks down the hallway and enters the room where the infant is screaming.

The infant is contained in a crib inside the empty white room.

The man approaches the crib and peers inside. With compassion, he scoops the infant in his fingertips. Comforting its uneasiness.

The man slowly walks to the window, *look at what beauty. Do you want to be a part of it?*

He glances down at the child observing it. He notices a sort of green seeping from the infant's left nostril. He attempts to wipe it with his fingers, but the seepage continues.

He looks at the child again.

The infant's head collapses inward.

Vulgar Persons —
A man is walking at dusk hitch-hiking.
He is picked up by someone driving a World War II army truck. He hops inside the back and gets comfortable. He looks to his right. A stranger is covered by an olive-green army blanket. Out of curiosity, he scoots closer to the stranger and lifts the cover off his face. The stranger responds "I am glad you came along, friend. Now, be kind. Remove the cover."

The man removes the blanket to find that the stranger is naked. Except for his genitalia, which is encased in a leather studded casing with a hole in the middle. So that his penis may protrude.

The man being uncomfortable veils his eyes. The stranger orders the man to look at him. The man hesitantly looks.

The stranger prepares himself for a rigorous custom of courtship and becomes physically knotted with the man. The stranger forces the man to copulate with him. While doing so the man struggles to free himself. Holding up the stranger's legs he pushes away.

The man looks up and sees himself sitting in the place of the stranger.

Old Men Gather —
A fellow looks up and he is holding his leg over his head. He looks around.

Children are seated all around him. So, he repositions himself in a Lotus. He solely gazes at the glare in the children's eyes.

A child approaches the fellow in tears, complaining of his incapability to urinate.
The fellow encourages the child to try. The child stresses the common signs of urination. The child begins to scream in pain and begins defecating from his penis.

Circus music lingers in the background.

NORTH [depart]

"Time has no mercy. It's there. It stays still or it moves.
And you're there with it. Staying still or moving with it.
I think it moves. And we move with it. And keep moving."
– Simon J. Ortiz, *Time as Memory as Story*

Gahé Dził / Mountain Spirits

always for my family

Circling round flames and dancing with the blazes
Encumbering sparks take flight into the night sky,
A swirling twinkle resembling a star crown
Moving into empty canopies resembling ghosts

A threshold colossal structure with rusty bells shakes
the sound of fire sings lingering beyond the flames
sent across the mountains and valleys

These spirits come from the mountains and move towards
the south, between the sacred narrow canyons,
The Sierra Madre Canyon walls sing in their echoes

A medicine reveals a stick and brings the wall down
For the Ndé – the people who wandered into night
Ascending towards the ending sky and onto the lost land

Losing their tongues and eyes they consume the mountain
Air and waters trying to heal all their lungs that bellowed
Outward against the slow breezes and heavy breaths

For a hundred years, the spirits protected them from
the sixteenth calvary who then believed, in all their hearts,
a good Injun was a dead Injun. Even then the spirits protected
the people for another twenty-seven years until they reached
                              —their forced destination

A place where cutting their hair died as the spirits watched
The people searched the underground catacombs of St. Augustine
While hearing the waves crash against the stone walls

Outside the thick walls, the people were exposed
To yellow fever and malaria, they died and died

                    —some survived

After thirty more years, the people returned to their homeland
closer to the Skeleton Canyons where an epic scribed
on the mountain walls called back their ancestors

At night the drumming echoed like the murmur inside
Their bodies hearing the loud thumps come and go

In 1986 the people returned to their original place
                        —entering ancient canyons
                        —honoring those killed
                        —remembering mountains

At night the sparks fly high as the people hear those rusty bells
and hollow songs   —they feel the drums and footsteps
reverberate
Inside their veins every time, they look to the mountains

I Looked at Those Pictures
for Pauline M. and Fred M. Jr.

Your soft hand — waves before the blurred blue of expression.
Your soft hand — lays below the guardian boulders, not moving,

Your young body — dances with others on a clifftop.
Your young body — outstretched on the ground covered in a
casing of dry mud.
Your young body — piled beneath the cusp of a ravine, mixed
with part earth, part pebbles, and part twigs.

Your feet were running — dash upon the darkening walls of fading
arroyos.
Your feet were running — left for dead inside the cradling desert along the
roadway.
                            — at the peak of the night.

Nadlé freely wavers with the self — continually changing.
Nadlé freely wavers among self — and the Holy Ones.
Nadlé loosely sprinkles pollen— upon the place where
        the ghost weed grows.

Clouds and sky — look upon your landscape of celestial rest.
Clouds and sky — gaze upon the blaze of morning mist,
        as you exist within your unmoving solitude.

The juniper, cedar, and sand — sift through your delicate wake.
The juniper, cedar, and sand — save the Night Way passage
        towards your ascension inside the scattering stars.

I looked at those pictures and saw you lying there.

I looked at those pictures and saw myself.
        I looked at those pictures …

Elements

fire snaps, flames rush
as swirling features, lighting their faces
and capturing their movement
Sparks fly into the wielding darkness,
combining with stars and the night sky,
as it was since the beginning

blending with the spread of brilliant specks
the sparks spin with dark liberty,
then fly with the embrace of our people,
where they wait for the arrival
      'iłk'idánde   the beginning —

the drum is the pulse
inside the veins and feet
the song is the breath
inside the mouth
the blood is deliverance
inside the prayers

it is a heartbeat
it is a song
it is a prayer
it is a spark
gliding into the face of that scattering brilliance

standing inside memory,
through the eyes of mothers,
whose same eyes signal their emergence
from each preceding world

the dancers dance with demonstrations
toward spirits and face the loss inside
the recognizable features of landscape and skin

piercing the hollow spaces,
piercing the hollow stares

de tááł	dancing
haadúú'ą	singing
'itedadli	praying

until sunrise —

in a slow-motion sway
following one another in a succinct
motion blur holding a place at the drum
securing a location to fire and sky

white is the sacred color of breath
yellow is the birth of the Eastern light
blue is the stone sacred as water
green is the skin for sheltering the lives
black is the unavoidable end and the beginning

sunrise —

chish diłtłi	standing with smells of cinder
ku hutas	running with ghosts of fire
shi haadúú'ą gúnyuł	singing with gusts of air
shi 'ik l'idá beedaajindánde	glaring with the eye sights
ha'úú'ą neełdą guuk'as	waiting for the sun after a cold night

the rays penetrate and embrace the instance
where voices feel the shaking skin
the day begins with a song
another instance of feeling each step beneath
the feet and recognize the dance

a rhythm fuses the fibers of history to culture
bounding each step to deviating acts of violence

dancing against a forbidden possibility
of the existence   of prejudice —
of inevitable invasiveness
                    of dance —

the movements are unending,
defining the back-and-forth voyage
through the night air

the blare of the straining night
beside the sacred mountains
though strands of vast cricket songs
singing along like wisps of wind
twirling off into the stars and rejoining the constellations
continuing the flight of sparks to a place in perpetuity

Expectations
for Boris Pinkerton

today I look for you —
I walk from room to room

the floors of the house still creak
and Ms. Bird still coos from her cage

there have been a few nights
where I caught you in the corner of my eye
but when I turn —

the expectation hastens

less the red clay from your origin
                                        Pavilion —
the small quiet town, where you were born

the days and nights haunt
the places where we tread
but pieces of your existence
are carefully tucked quietly away
in corners of each empty room

no one knows how to comfort death
because it does not soothe the self or soul
it only binds us tighter to the everlasting cord

so now you live upon the dresser
in a fancy wooden urn
lacquered as a mirror
and your impression pressed into clay
still leaves us in dismay

a periphery can make great friends or worse
enemies but I still look for you

Journey

your body curls
suggesting
you may be leaving soon

your name   — a voyage
finding a destination away from here
                a daunting city

knowing the simplicity of being
and pacifying your loyal wildings
always searching inside for life
only discovering the purpose
of your name implying travel

but the name also means company
without a compelling obligation

the emergency sirens
wail outside in the night sky

you sing to tune your heart
and soothe the dying souls
passing unknowingly by

now your heart and body
summon the heavy tumors
but time does not matter anymore

                        — you are on your way

dying was not our choice of remedy
to perpetuate the inevitable
to think that a moment is chosen
                — to move beyond

the afterlife quietly and now
where will you now go?
— who will be your master?

Secret Rain
for P. Mitchell

the rise of the day begins remotely
against orange mesas
her gaze escapes distant mountains
insects and chirping spaces

a mesa's crest obscures the eyes
as the clouds move about
by the thief's murderous action
whom he intends
to leave her life without

a cloud rises high in a collection
as rain feeds the flowers
a violent display in action
removes all remaining hours

a release of dust in time decays
mirrors the earth of mud
washing of hands, feet, face, and disdain
turning water into blood

Constellation

happening in a small room, in the back
of an empty building, at the center of Denver,
leaving a sloppy recognition on my face

standing in a room at night with my other self,
a spatial moment of recollection and reflection

astride in my walk leading me to a large city,
forgetting a star dream of mothers
who search longingly for their desperate sons

turning my head weeping, covering my eyes
from all past midnight skies and colors carving out mesas
remembering days of stolen celestial memories,
and persistent confessions

lost among conversation, and the smell
of nicotine on the fingers, falling into a differential
phase of lunar refraction, a plate glass scattering
about the floor, an irretrievable feeling of mist still
lingering as fragments and sickness

raining a few days ago, and leaving the streets,
an exuding cluster of displaced recluse stars
rendering a meld of structure into an ocular madness
and compromises the wills of prevailing sinners
attempting to coexist in a space as two bodies

after leaving this gathering of bodies and exiting
the building, forgetting about flailing my desires
walking the streets of this glistening city
discovering myself staring at another ceiling
of luminescent stars trailing back to me

a concealing constellation where I await the discovery
of another bed not meant for sleeping but for traveling
                                        – alone

seemingly shell-shocked not for the sake of war
but for the chance of meeting anyone in a meaningless
face where everyone is standing ever closer,
as cigarette smoke in the night sky

Standing Reflection

a child stands in reflection   longing to be
gazing behind eyes longing in mounts of fear

a dying person, old and worn, all that is seen
life chases a dream but fails to view

within a blind shimmer   always standing near
the person is reminded of the child who comes to be

can the person accept the gift of sight that lies internally?
facing a choice of the light within, not seen so clearly

can a child, so young and free, embrace a sight to see?
the child stands near the dying person, a tear on each face

grieving is an honest regard, recognition is the mirror
a child standing in reflection, learning to be

after much strife and ache the person has come to see
 that a child has stood nearby and remained sincere

a child can now embrace the dying person soon-to-be
the person is lifted high above the need for reprieve

though in an act of haste displaying a calm demur
the child standing in a reflection wants to be a person

living, not dying which is what each remains to see

Prisoner

to whom I am not blood born — binding eyes shut
to whom I un-connect with in my life
to whom I did not offer a heart — [un-reciprocal]

he sits every evening and eats at the same table
his wicked silence consumes the directional fingers

his routine instills fear, impeding those around him
his solution turns at every strap

he dismisses himself after each meal
and empties his life down a can
he sips and recoils uttering whispers
                    — *not good enough*

            rain dampens his hair threatening
his pride while the grass drowns outside

he upholds an uncaring stare that saturates
his pupils, concealing him in a tunnel view

he commands his long-ago child in any direction
            hiding inside suspicions of a corroding mirror
            and vainly announcing his arrival

he hears the cold granite scrambling his name
he dreams away the ease of stressing syllables,
            drink now… home… grave… amend… drip/drown…

his death is a declaration of choice, no movement
            limp head… limp face… limp hands… limp feet…

his stagnant impulse obscures the existence of Christ
his callousness buries the layers of salvation

every steeping drip in brown bottles
he carries a sordid vessel leaving him vacant
his blood murmurs a lonely child in the hallway

— a medicine man casually offers a ritual
— a door is now unsolemn and measured
— a door to his room slowly shuts

to whom I unwillingly still write eulogies for

Ghost Hands

electric water stirs in a cup
tilting the cross-shape ridges
on her face

a pleating notion placed
there for her recognition
a speck of ancient dirt appears
on her hands and arm

— paper   — ink   — paintbrush
each contraption becomes a secondary object
coffee cups and cigarettes seem to disappear

whatever happened to the Corvair wagon?

eroding eyes appear sunken in soils
behind a church renovation
where dreams are kept
Sunday morning the church bell rings
sounds vibrate and trickle down
the old cracks in adobe walls

standing naked in the absence
of negative and positive poles
holding a crutch to her breast
hiding a physical fetal position
        concluding with an afterlife
        concluding nothing as a place
        concluding something written
        concluding some things are everything

symbolically sleeping
        —while a sign reads, *Employees Only*

North American Epitaph on the Doctrine of Discovery

[...] ~~we therefore are rightly led, and hold it as our duty, to grant you even~~
~~of our own accord and in your favor those things whereby with effort each~~
~~day more hearty you may be enabled for the honor of God himself and the~~
~~spread of the Christian rule to carry forward your holy and praiseworthy~~
~~purpose so pleasing to immortal God.~~

> — Pope Alexander VI. <u>Demarcation Bull Granting</u>
> <u>Spain Possession of Lands Discovered by</u>
> <u>Columbus</u> Rome, May 4, 1493.

to damn a lie in ~~God's~~ name, for the blood
of the first people, will not suffice to the extent
of loss of life

> — equals wealth

though ~~Heaven~~ cannot replace the land or lives
stolen through professional colonial acts justified
on bearing a heavy cross

> — despite all impious

generosity and kindness, ~~His~~ name does not rationalize
the irremediable crimes that make those sacrosanct
similarities just

> — and human begets human

what is all to gain, if not more blood?

"there is light there"

the ray is a bringer   inside the beginnings
of possibilities and a harvester of colors

in its absence there is always a presence
peering through a fluttering curtain   shedding
its color from the body   into the shadow

casting the everlasting shade upon
the rusty canyon walls and cascade of skyscrapers

the ever-transitioning gray shade and enveloping
Indigo is what is left for each given possibility

the possibility to see others and even ourselves
casting the long desperate shadows bending
into scrupulous form reaching   for embrace

bodies are lost in the tangibility of the darkness
— maybe, that is the result of why limbs reach

[there is light there]

from umbra to penumbra drawing specific definitions
of what is forming because of the concurrent illumination

the movements in each are because the   sun rotates
         the   moon rotates
the stars taking a millennium to cast that momentary gleam
so the surging energy can begin in the dances
the songs
the incantations

— syzygy —

the weight of reflection reminds the eyes to seek
what is behind the mind   so a spark can be lit

a dawn for what can be expected   in a yucca basket or
buckskin pouch   summoning the blessings
and gazing through all awaiting pollen of bodies

finally, sprouting from seed and from water   where all
stems travel through the soil
in all illumination

bursting through germination
which turns into a dangerous determination

so many cannot be cared for
so many cannot be recognized
never finding their opposite

waters will flow and fall   fauna and seasons will cycle
feet will tread and dance   into the night and welcome the
morning, there is   an absence of opposites
as long as the search for each other never ceases

[there is light there]

Acknowledgements

Always thanks to my spouse Todd and my family in Mescalero, Tó 'hajiileé, and Lakewood, The Publishing Triangle, Colorado Authors League (CAL), Colorado Poets Center (CPC), the Twenty Bellows editors, Allison Adele Hedge Coke, Travis Hedge Coke, Julian Talamantez Brolaski, Heather Ahtone-Begaye, tanner menard, Dean Rader, James Thomas Stevens, Arthur Sze, David Mason, Silvia Canton Rondoni, Charlotte Gullick, Ursula Pike, Bobby LeFebre, Melvern Books, Tim Roberts, & Counterpath, Brice Maiurro, the South Broadway Press editors, Todd Herman, & eastwindow gallery, Jake Skeets, Matson (Melinda) Spina, Lynnette Haozous, Christopher Nelson, & Green Linden Press, Beatrice Szymkowiak, Adam Day & Action Spectacle, Sarah Herrin, & Beyond the Veil Press, Headroom Sessions, Serena Chopra, Hillary Leftwich, Aerik Francis, John Patsynski, Ahja Fox, Erika Wurth, Michael Wendt, & Woodland Patterns, Kimberly Blaeser, Kinsale Drake, Margo Tamez, Craig Svonkin, Theresa Crater, Kathryn Winograd, George Cramer, Vincent Hostak, & the Phantom Script, Franco Viviani, Radha Marcum, & Poet to Poet, Justin Veach, & the Longmont Museum, Ellen G. Stone, Wendy Videlock, Tessa Kale, Valerie Szarek, Beth Franklin, Steven Law, & Poetry Snaps, Andrew Zichosch, & his classmates at Sky Ranch Middle School, B.A.Van Sise, the editors at THE WILD WORD.

Grateful acknowledgments are made to the editors of the following publications and persons. Which earlier versions & titles of the following work, first appeared:

MTV: *Gahé Dził/Mountain Spirits* (early '90s version)
Academy of American Poets-Poem A Day: *Gahé Dził / Mountain Spirits*
Voices of Thunder: *Self Portrait Before Candlelight, He is Dead Haastįń 'ánesitįįń/Prisoner*
MetroSphere vol. 27: *Open Road*
MetroSphere vol 28: *Scarce Seeds*
MetroSphere/Collections vol. 30: *Ha'úú'a/Sunrise, Tonight, Bruise, I Looked at Those Pictures, San Francisco 1962* (early version)
Future Earth Magazine vol. 5: *San Francisco California 1962, Long*

Distant Travel

Infectious Hope, Anthology: *A Prayer for Them*

Twenty Bellows: *Thorax and Wean, Orchid Moon, Momentary* Thin Air
Magazine: *Calm, Creating Golden Heliotropes In His Hands*

Dwell Anthology (South Broadway Press): *Moonlit Slabs of Light on a Hernandez Church Floor*

South Broadway Ghost Society Press, online reprint: *Moonlit Slabs of Light on a Hernandez Church Floor*

Under A Warm Green Linden, num. 14, (Green Linden Press): *Elements, Long Distance Traveling*

We Apologize For The Inconvenience: Queer and Trans Voices, Club Q Anthology (Beyond The Veil Press): *Come On Up To The House*

Action, Spectacle Magazine, summer 2023 issue: *Random Thought Patterns / Anatomy of a Lipid Cell*

Fungi Magazine: vol. #, Summer 2023 issue: *Stasis*

New Feather: (Winter Issue), November 6, 2023 - *Illusion of Dreams & Existence*

Yellow Medicine Review, Fall 2023: *Wake, Expectations, Elements* (anthologized print)

On the National Language: The Poetry of America's Endangered Tongues, B.A. Van Sise, *"there is light there"*

The Wild Word, LIVE #78-Summer 2024-Final Issue, *Always Asphalt*

About the Author

Crisosto Apache is from Mescalero, New Mexico, on the Mescalero Apache reservation. Crisosto is Mescalero Apache, Chiricahua Apache, and Diné (Navajo) of the Salt Clan, born for the Towering House Clan. Apache attended and earned an MFA at the Institute of American Indian Arts (IAIA) and is an Associate Professor of English and Creative Writing. Crisosto is also an editor-at-large for The *Offing* Magazine. Apache's books are ~~GENESIS~~ (Lost Alphabet) & *Ghostword* (Gnashing Teeth Publishing), winner of the Publishing Triangle's 2023 Betty Berzon Emerging Writers Award and a finalist for the 2023 Colorado Authors League Award in poetry. Apache is also a two-time Pushcart Prize nominee.

Discussion Questions
by Tiffany Woodley

1. The cover photo is Crisosto Apache's inspiration for this collection. Take a minute to inhabit the image and consider the title. How do these two connect to what you've experienced on the pages within?

2. The first section of this collection is East [wake]. Which types of awakenings are most notable?

3. "A Prayer for Us" feels very similar to the ancient Greek tradition of Calling the Muse while instead invoking the natural world. How does the poem (perhaps the work as a whole) serve to honor nature?

4. "Born for Thorax" and "On Speaking" utilize artistic spacing which appear throughout the rest of the collection. What thoughts fill these empty spaces for you?

5. The South section is driven by the idea of arrivals, but also the cyclical nature of revision and growth. What kinds of knowledge develop over this section?

6. Apache uses repetition as a vehicle for key moments in pieces like "San Francisco, California 1962", "Wake" and "Snow Falling in C Minor". Discuss how he uses this tool to emphasize elements of the pieces. Try exploring the varying effects of different types of repetition.

7. The poem "Dyad" is built in two columns which opens up different ways to read the piece. Try out reading the poem straight across, then each column one at a time. Which reading resonates more with you?

8. In the preface, the author says that his work investigates "what the poem 'is' about in a state of 'meaningfulness', presence, and moments." Which moments are you finding yourself caught up in?

9. Crisosto's poetry often integrates the surreal; in what ways does the West section feel like a dream sequence?

10. "Random Thought Patterns / Anatomy of a Lipid Cell", "Diminishing Spaces Between A Mouth" and "Self Portrait Before Candlelight" each use the em dash punctuation. How does its use impact the flow and meaning of the poems?

11. Look back at some of the poems that are dedicated to particular people. Which relationships are honored and which are tested? Which ones feel like relationships in your life?

12. The poet makes a departure for the final part of the book through his reference to the North. What will you depart the work with?